MY LIFE'S JOURNEY...

Nate Robinson

My Life's Journey...

Author: Nate Robinson

Published by Austin Brothers Publishing

Keller, Texas

www.austinbrotherspublishing.com

ISBN 978-0-9903477-1-2

This and other books published by

Austin Brothers Publishing can be purchased at

www.austinbrotherspublishing.com

Printed in the United States of America

2014 -- First Edition

*"And not to live by the white men's myths (not to re-
ject those too-clear eyes, but not to long for them,
or see through their blue distances all colors but my
own)."*

Reginald Shepherd

Contents

Forword

Have you ever struggled or felt like life is all together too hard? In that struggle have you ever felt like you can't find the words to express what you are feeling? Have you ever been around someone who you know is in a lot of pain, but you feel like you can't fully understand them? Well, *My Life's Journey...* is a great book to read. It truly is a universal book that all can relate to.

Being only thirteen months younger than my brother, Nathan Robinson offered me a unique perspective on his life. I watched him go through an intense inner struggle to find a purpose for life. During this time, he was hard to be around and he felt like no one understood him, but one thing he could and would do was write. I remember sitting in the living room with my mom and younger brother while Nathan read poems he had written. We felt like he was given a gift to express the deep questions many seem to have in this life, but cannot find the words to express them.

During this time I wondered if my brother was ever going to make it out of this perpetual state of pessimism because he seemed to have only tough questions, but no real answers. However, through a set of divine circumstances he started channeling this very negative questioning into something positive. He finally felt like he was getting some answers. He began to fuel that energy into making something of himself that would better the society around him.

Looking back, my brother's transformation was a big one. It was like he had traveled through the dark and dingy dungeons of his heart and gone almost to the point of no return, but miraculously made it out. He went from someone parents did not want their children to be around to someone parents desired their children to be around.

Now my brother still has questions, but it's a different sort of questions. It's the type of questions that come from having hope not despair; trust not fear; love not hate. I know you will enjoy walking this journey alongside my brother as you read his heartfelt collection of inspired poems.

I am very thankful to have a brother like Nathan, who was not afraid to ask the hard questions, but learned how to turn it into something positive. I know his journey is not over, and to be honest, I am glad it's not. There are still many answers out there for him and all of us to find in this life, and I am grateful that he will keep searching until he finds them.

Naomi Howell
Nate's Sister

Introduction

My Life's Journey… is a book of poetry that tries to display the inner-struggle of my life between the ages of 18 and 23. The book is set up as a progression through maturity during that period of my life. It is separated into three sections (Questioning, Answers, and Questions) to show the mental, emotional, and spiritual growth during that time in my life.

The first section, "Questioning," is a collection of poems that are arranged in such a way to show the reader the questioning of my purpose in life and internal and external struggles that resulted from those questions. That was a very confusing and isolated period of time for me, and this set of poems brings that to life.

The second section is called "Answers." These poems show some of that frustration and confusion being channeled in a positive way through creative expression. Also some of these poems exemplify a spiritual side of me that is starting to play a dominant role in my perception on life and what is going on around me.

The third section is called "Questions." Although I found some answers, they only brought more questions that needed to be answered to my heart. These poems display to the reader a more complex and more mature expression of my struggle that I face internally with myself, the world around me, with God, and where I stand with him.

The title of this book *My Life's Journey...* has the ellipsis after it because it symbolizes that my life's journey is not over. The title says that this is what I have come up with so far. It is my hope that some of these poems can be felt in the hearts of the people who read them, because that is where all of these poems were written from—my heart.

Nate Robinson

Chapter One
Questioning

Darkness cannot drive out darkness; only light can do that. Hate cannot drive out hate; only love can do that.

Dr. Marin Luther King Jr.

Set Me Free

06/04/2003

Set me Free - so I can grow into who I am supposed
to be

Set me Free - because my mind is caged down by
the expectations of this society

I hurt inside, but I can't show my feelings

Because, what's the point - when the people I'm
dealing with don't have the capacity in their
brain to feel me

Set me Free - because all I've ever seen was
negativity

So much so, that I thought that what I saw was
what I am supposed to be

People judge me based on what they can see,

They don't consider that what they haven't seen or
what they don't see on the inside of me, is really
who I am

Set me Free - because unconditional love is
something I have never experienced

I might look mad, but I am really jealous

Because knowing that I never had true love makes
me furious,

I'm curious about this world outside of what I see

　　　　　　　　　　　　　　　　Nate Robinson

But coming to the realization that when I was born
   - success was not expected,

Because of my parents poverty

It's gonna take more to set me free, than these up
   tight white people with degrees. Who think that
   they really know everything about me. Trying to
   assess and evaluate why I am the way I am.

You see I am not all of the other thugs and
   hoodlums that come from where I live

I'm different, yet for me to accept your help,

First I need to be sure that you want to help me
   because you truly want to give

I don't need some snobby, "I think I know
   everything," type person who already has made
   up his/her mind about who I am

Or some rich person using me for a reason to show
   his/her friends that he/she can do something
   good in the world by acting like he/she is helping
   some kid turn his/her life around

I don't need that and I don't want that,

Because I see right through your BS

And that is what you are to me,

You are full of BS

You don't know me

You don't really want to know me

Because you deprive me of the one thing that I've
   needed the most my whole life, LOVE

Set me Free - because I don't have that many
    positive role models who are willing to look
    me in the eyes and tell me the right way to do
    things

Set me Free - because I have the potential to be a
    great person,

I am more than what it says about me in their
    writings

Set me Free - because deep down inside, I am not
    free, and it is my wish to truly be free

I Nathan Robinson can say these words in truth

Because not that too long ago this cry from
    someone's heart was the cry that used to come
    from me

Nate Robinson

Confusion

12/04/2002

I'm goin' down

I'm going down staircases at a time with an
accelerating speed

As the speed inclines

I lose more of my right mind

Because there is no time - to think

Or blink

The stage is set and I can feel the performer in me
rise to the occasion

The audience is in anticipation for the man of the
hour

He's been through so much agony and frustration in
his life that he can't even describe his feelings

His heart is full of pain that doesn't seem to want
to go away

Have you ever felt that no one in this world can
feel the pain you feel in your heart at this exact
moment?

Have you had dreams that describe what you wish
would happen in your circumstance,

But when reality sets in the dream becomes unreal
and it laughs at you teasing you with it's fake
relevance to your situation?

Have you ever loved something so much that you would die for it?

That you would go through being humiliated for, and made fun of for, and stabbed in the back for?

Have you ever wanted to cry so hard that you couldn't cry because the pain in your heart is numb to emotion because the feeling is just that intense?

Know that I am your God and I am not someone who would lie to you

Know that I will never leave you nor forsake you

Know that I will see you through until the end

Can you believe in what you can't see?

Can you believe that what you can't see has control over everything that goes on in this planet?

Why does pain come?

Why does the dagger stay in my heart?

I want them to feel the pain that I feel

I want to be able to express the emotions that run through my blood

I want to succeed

But what is success?

Nate Robinson

Make me what ever you
want to make me

07/24/2000

God,

Make me whatever you want me to be

I surrender my life,

And lay it at your feet

I bend my knees humbly asking,

Lord,

Do you really love me after all I've done?

Even though sometimes I stay away from fun

I run, but only to you

Because of what's happening,

I feel I can only trust few

As far as people are concerned

So many times,

I just get burned

Am I wrong for not followin' the crowd

I stand alone,

With you as my shield

When it is time

You'll let me know

So until then,

Make me whatever you want to make me

Nate Robinson

Da Inner Struggle

07/25/1999

I feel like no love is lost, yet no love is gained

The crazed out thoughts in my head, is all that
remain

I'm insane,

Brotha, you need your mind rearranged

What's wrong is I'm workin' for chump-change

But they still look at me strange

No matter what the heck I do

I need to leave them fools alone and start lovin' you

But who am I talkin' to?

It ain't like all this stuff I'm doin' is brand new

Tell me who can I trust and where can I go to?

When it's ashes to ashes and all of these people are
see through

Somebody help me I'm bleedin

'Cause time don't stop it just keeps on proceedin

I'm in a boxing ring with Satan and he's got me in a
corna

I know I could get out

But the scary part is I don't think I wanna

It's either live or die - the choice is up to me

Go to heaven or hell - so what's it gonna be?

He's askin' - why are you takin chances when he is
   talkin eternity?

No love is lost - No love is gained

The crazed out thoughts in my head - is all that
   remain

                                    Nate Robinson

My Path

09/02/1999

I'm feelin' like I'm one of a kind

    And searching to find

The answer to all my questions,

    It's got me stressin', and my patience is runnin thin

I need to look within,

    And then realize

That everything I do must be in disguise

Act wise and instead be a humble person

    Get rid of all this confusion and disbelief

Stop relentless searchin'

    And go to God for my fresh sense of relief

Don't retreat and accept defeat

But move forward,

    Knowing your enemy can be beat

I wanna be able to stand stress and thought free

    Every word means something

I need to check me

And look underneath for everything I think that I'm missin'

    Be simple and plain

And quit all this dissin'

Not be aware of what's constantly goin' on around
me

Stand strong and firm

Like the great evergreen tree

Be an unmovable object

For those who would try and inspect my project

Because we as people all have dreams

No matter how bad it seems

I want to be a free-flowin' stream

That teams up with a whole bunch of others

To make the Pacific

'Cause through him, we are all brothers

Stress, is something that wears on my mind

Time and time again

In order to win

We can't sin and gotta be friends

But we were born sinners

And through the friends I've had

There ain't no real winners

All I can do is believe,

And retrieve all the broken pieces of my heart

Through faith and hard work

It's guaranteed to start

                                         Nate Robinson

What I'm doin'

Is making an unbreakable foundation

   So when tested

I already know what I'm facin'

You Gotta Have Faith

09/08/1999

I'm feelin' like my destiny is complexity

    and everyone who is next to me is guessin' me

Why? 'Cause everything ain't that serious

    The thoughts in my head are enough to drive
    anyone delirious

I'm curious about my future

I know it's in God's hands

    I feel like every time I gotta chance - it

Reading my mind is a strange thing to do

    'Cause every word I say I want to be true

Who are you to tell me I am crazy?

    Why can't you let the one who made me call me
    crazy?

My thoughts are hazy and clouded

    I ain't got to prove to nobody - I'm bout it

I wish God would reveal his plan to me

    That way I would not feel like everything is
    fantasy

Reality - got me trippin

    Instead of slippin I am flippin the script

And exceptin lip, so I can kick my pride to the curb

Nate Robinson

Not thinkin' bout people gettin' what they deserve

Have you heard the word and the verdict

God is settin up shop

While the demon's thoughts was twisted and perverted - for Nate

And I anticipate and wait for the lord to set me free

But maybe I'm already free and the Lord has used the key

To unlock the inner spirit within me

If that's the case why do I worry?

And feel that everything must be done in a hurry?

My vision is blurry, so I scurry to my next destination

Knowing I can't wait before it's too late

So I try and run without hesitation

This situation has got me pacin'

While the devil is givin chasin'

I steady hope for sensation and run away from temptation

Not knowing what I am facin' I gotta have patience and have faith

That he knows what he's doin'

With him I am never losin'

Put my focus on him and concentrate

From: The student

To: The Teacher

06/22/2000

Help me ta grow

And help me ta understand and know

All that you want to show

Take me to a place where only few go

Because I wanna sport your logo

I believe in you

And that what you say is true

Make me in your image

So what I say will be what I do

I want levels of intimacy that very few reach

I want to be annointed like you were

To teach how you teached

And to preach how you preached

Give me love and passion

To stir up your army

Give me your power and authority

So no demons can harm me

Let everything I do be done for your glory

And let it touch heaven with every additional story

 Nate Robinson

I wanna heal the sick and see the impossible done

In Jesus name

    I proclaim with a loud voice

And all of Satan's angels run

Not for fun but for the Son

The Son of the living God

The God who raised Jesus from the dead

The God who made Moses a leader and head

Make me that man

Who is hip to all of your plans

What I Ask of You

06/27/2000

Forgive me oh Lord

For I am a sinner

But through the blood of your son

I can be made whole and transformed into a winner

Your grace and mercy are so hard to comprehend

Help me,

because I sometimes struggle with this thing called
   sin

I cannot fend for myself

I call upon your name to ensure my spiritual health

I desperately need your strength for sudden urges

   of sexual thoughts that haunt my mind

Save me from my flesh and give me a new heart

   with good eyes well shaped and refined

No more excuses and lines

Gotta keep movin' and stop listening to the devil's
   lies

I want to fight the good fight like Paul

   Be able to conquer the power of sin

So I can once and for all jump its wall

Without lookin back

                                    Nate Robinson

I want to be through with that

'Cause sin is something we must fight and conquer everyday

and the power in Jesus Christ to fight it

represents our only way

To enjoy true victory

So man of God

I command my Jesus inside to come alive in me

To kill the enemy until he cannot breathe

I receive your treatment and ask for your help

To digest solid spiritual food you give me to eat

I can't think quick, but must think slow to process

To enable everything that has been taught to me the opportunity to digest

Can't rest 'cause the devil doesn't

Right when I thought the war was over it really wasn't

When's it my turn

07/27/2000

When's it gonna be my turn to see a little success

Seem that the bad people end up with the best

My stress

I guess, that love wants to take her precious time

As I wait impatiently for my find

    I bend but don't fold

Won't give up, but feel old and rolled on

My past is just a forgotten memory

    People have come and gone so fast

This is all so new to me

'Cause now I play a different game

In which all I feel is internal and inexpressible pain

I ain't playin' as I anticipate the gift of mercy

Why is it that I feel that everyone is out to hurt me?

Desert me, when all I want is peace

and everyone to be honest and real

But if I am not these things above

Then guess how dat make me feel

    What the deal

I get ill thinkin 'bout my current situation

Nate Robinson

    It's scary to me

I'm gettin' used to frustration

Temptation got a tight grip

and just won't seem to let go

    I'm too cold to trip, but sometimes I slip

'Cause the Lord's plan is so slow

My Learning Process

These questions in my head make me ponder

Whether or not I even care if I'm a gonner

This mental drama couldn't be normal

I can't and don't want it to

But it's all a part of what I must go through

To see the promised land

You have to be willing to be the goat if you want to
be the hero

Plus, you can't skip any numbers

You've got to start at zero

So as long as he's controllin'

I've got to be patient and endure

Because then his plans will keep on rollin'

Man, it just hurts inside

My pride, if I had any left

Suicide, with my mental's death

This stagnation in my life, why can't it just go away?

All my words are so simple now, and why is it so
hard to pray?

Yet so easy to stray

Away from the truth

 Nate Robinson

I feel like I need proof

Proof of his existance

'Cause in an instance

My resistance, could be my life's sentence

What team do I join?

I'm sick and tired of being the middle man

Take a hint and stick with it

But sometimes I don't think I can, be a man

What would a man do?

If he is true and all of his plans just fall through

On top of that, can't nobody see you

A crew, is a thing of the past

I run solo, with or without the pack

My back can be watched by me and only me

That's how I feel

Now that I've got my dose of reality

My Prayer

08/23/2000

Lord

I wanna be about you

I want to do what you want me to do

Not be about show

or having anything to do with hurting people that
    don't know

I want to sell out for you

Sacrifice everything I have for the sake of you

Give me a passion to read your word

    Give me discernment to know when to cut

So the wicked get what they deserve

I want to be used for that purpose

Not abuse what you've given me

I understand that vengeance is yours

Help me to hold my tongue in situations of stress

Help me to show the world that it's not just about
    how you dress

Let me do something fresh

Something different

I'm holdin' on to you through the storm

Bring me to the place where like Job

Nate Robinson

No matter what happens my heart towards you will
always remain warm

Don't need fancy words or slang

Just need to know and understand that you are
stronger than any man or gang

You came for everyone

From the worst of people to the best

You used your son for my sins

So I could have the opportunity to be blessed

I humble myself for your promises and for your
glory

I die to my flesh in order for you to make up this
story

Without faith it's impossible to please God

Without what Christ did we'd have no way to
escape the wrath of God

Take me through whatever it takes to become that
man

I now know that it's gonna be pain, and without
you it's impossible to stand

Don't let me get big and forget about who
delivered me

It's because of you I live

And because of what Christ did that makes me
worthy

I cherish you and although I might make mistakes

You said you'll bring me through

No matter what I do

Because of your mercy and grace

                                        Nate Robinson

Taking the proper steps

09/06/2000

I wanna grow

    Not to show

But to glow in your sight

I wanna fight for what I know is right

Teach me Lord how to walk in your ways

Show me who you are in my short length of days

I want to chase after righteousness

I want to be full of your Holy Spirit

    I want to walk in proper alignment

So there is no way the devil can clear it

I want to slay the devil when I pray

I want the Holy Spirit directing every word I say

I want to be satisfied with little or plenty

Not worryin' about where I am or where I could be

But simply holdin' on to you

    Pilin' scriptures in my heart

So I am not one of the slew

Few are chosen, yet many are called

Those many must try and face the devil in their
flesh, and end up beaten and mauled

I am under the protection of the blood of the lamb

No weapon formed against me shall prosper, not
    even Uncle Sam's

Lord, help me to understand the gospel

Then, we go from there

    Breathin' freely

'Cause I 'm redeemed by the blood and without a
    care

                              Nate Robinson

Turmoil

11/27/2000

I've seen a lot

Rolled with hoodies and preps

Stayed clean then sinned again while takin' life's
steps

Pushin reps, in the weight room and in the spirit

Readin' bible scriptures

By faith believin' I could cure it

What you hold dearest is easiest to forget

And everyone in this cruel world is fightin' for some
worthless respect

I detect the strangest of occurrences happenin' in
my mind

While tryin' to translate this rappin' and rewind my
time

But you can never get it back

I'm tryin' to use simple logic to figure out the facts

If there is a God then why does he love me?

And how am I as a believer supposed to open up
other people's eyes to see when I sometimes
struggle with reality?

In all actuality, I've fallen short of the glory of God

I can be a fake person and say that I've never been
    lost

I'm lookin' for the boss or whoever is runnin' this
    show

What if there isn't a God and this whole life is all
    about gettin' dough?

'Cause that's how some people is livin' their life

And who am I to tell them that what they doin' isn't
    right?

Look 'em in the eye and say that I have all the
    answers

When this thing called hard life is spreadin' like
    cancer

Good God, I got so much goin' on my brain

Yet only when I sin do I feel that earthly pain

I gain, then lose ground

I was lost, but now I'm found

Why God loves me, I don't know

Until I do, I'll believe in things unseen as if they
    were so

                                    Nate Robinson

Theory

12/04/2000

It started out when I was just a little seed

Found out that the world around me ain't bout
nothin' else but selfish greed

Then I was taught that you reap what you sow

So now I'm chillin' waitin' for when it's my time to
go

It's too slow

Intakin' theories bout this spirit called God

Holdin' on for dear life fightin' sin and believin'
there's a God

Resistin' temptation with all of my strength

Yet, it be some saints that be worried bout your
rank

What will it take to break the fake?

Will I be blessed in the end through faith?

Ain't tryin' to get caught up in a superhero status

Playin' on a team where everybody wants to be the
baddest

My saddest point so far is feelin' like I can't find the
bar

I got this mental scar and I am wonderin' why he
keeps startin' my car

'Cause it should be dead like I feel my life
    sometimes is

I want the truth and nothin' else but searchin' is
    losin' its fizz

God, if you up there, why do you care about me?

I'm readin' words on sheets of paper, but give me
    somethin' I can see

Tell me who am I supposed to be?

Or do I give up and except day-to-day livin' as my
    reality?

I wanna dream and I wanna dream big

At the same time, I am being weighed down with
    exceptin' life as it is

I want it to be perfect but will it ever happen?

I'm watchin old school movies and the fantasy is
    supposed to meet my satisfaction

My attraction is holdin' on to what I believe

But when I begin to doubt I feel like I've just been
    deceived

                                    Nate Robinson

My observations state this…

I got dreams that seem impossible to come true

I got ideas that deem colossal in the eyes of few

How does one take a chance at life?

When every single possibility goes against all logic
and responsibility?

I just wanna be free

Free from what, is the question

I'll start with having no fear of rejection or your
acceptance

Constant stressin' is a part of life

To get your blessin' some tears might go unwiped

I'm right when I say freedom comes from sacrifice

Just take a look at history, and how many people
have lost their life

Some could be dead and don't even know it

Bound by the bondages of livin' but to afraid to
show it

Some decide to quit and pay with the loss of the air
they breathe

Are they crazy?

Or is the internal torment that we all must face the
reason that they bleed?

FREE ME! FREE ME!

Is the cry of my inner soul

    The pain and frustration that comes with my
mental situation

Is what leads me to believe that I have little control

                    Nate Robinson

Searchin' for da real

03/11/2001

The question for today is why do we live?

If you don't know and understand your purpose for
livin' how much input and help can you give?

Questions that don't have answers are what haunt
and taunt me

Solutions to worldly problems that we all face are
where my serious thoughts be

Individuality is over-rated

How many people you know that say they love
themselves to death, but in all reality they really
hated it?

Stay frustrated, but try to act like they can't be
faded

Na man, I'm searchin' for some flat out real peace

The kind that never breaks no matter how many
hits it takes

Because the soul is content on the inside

Imitators of this trait ain't got nowhere to hide

You can try and use your pride and your muscle too

But if you ain't got real peace, try to look me in the
eye and tell me what you gonna do?

We're being handled and tossed to and fro

Is there a way out of this maze of confusion?

Nobody knows

'Cause nobody knows where it goes

Where it leads or where it ends

If nobody's right about why we're here

Then who's gonna be the one to set our minds and
the records clear?

Or are we so far gone that there's no way out?

And the only hope for an answer is death

Because we go through life with reasonable doubt

                                        Nate Robinson

This Is My Reality

I'm entering into worlds unknown

Does it make me crazy or mark my courage shown?

I feel all alone and at night I moan and groan

God please help me before my mind is blown

This is major I ain't talkin' bout no joke

What I'm doin' wasn't meant for just anyone
especially those who can't cope

With feeling like your bout to explode

    When knowin' you gotta be in patient mode

    and sometimes move as slow as the toad

When understandin' there's victory in the end

It hurts me inside departing with my only true
friend

    Will I win the war or just stay sore?

And struggle through the aftermath

    I see the open door and don't want pain no
more

So I pay attention to the chosen path

I got nothin' to lose in this game of spirits

And if you listen closely and be attentive you'll hear
it

The voice of the Most High talkin' through your
mind

I need to choose to fear it and get near it

When he's callin' me close to him

Run away from all evil and don't stay when I see
temptation

Right when I think I got it I'm brought down

And when I'm at the bottom he always seems to
come around

As intensity increases and my memories decrease

Causin' me to make up a thesis as I fall to my knees

Am I weak or awake?

Being real or actin' fake?

I got no time to debate

My whole existence is at stake

And if you can relate then please participate

    Before it's too late

    Ignore and feel the quake

'Cause everything is what you make it out to be

So open your eyes and see that even the rich are
livin' in poverty

Why does everyone got to fight to be number one?

We should all work together so the Lord can say, "A
job well done."

Sometimes I feel like everything is slippin' away

             Nate Robinson

When in reality does it mean that I'm searchin' for
    a better way?

I'm at the peak of nowhere

There ain't no real friends here

So I stay bold where it's cold and remain a leader
    not a follower

I wanna help ya not swallow ya

Tell me what's the difference between a hater and
    a man?

A hater wants damage when a man would take a
    stand and hold your hand

Not be reluctant when times get hard

Tell me, which card do I hold before I fold and grow
    old?

Love not hate and cherish before you perish

I got nothin' to lose, but I need someone to share
    with

Chapter Two

Answers

There is no better than adversity. Every defeat, every heartbreak, every loss, contains its own seed, its own lesson on how to improve your performance the next time.

Malcolm X

Da Real

07/25/2001

This is it, straight up no holds barred

The untamed explicit version of my heart that's
scarred

With no more regard to the possibility of hurtin'
others

Because the truth and nothin' but it

Is what I've been searchin' for to discover

It's a fact

Some say this and some say that

I choose to find my own way to expose the whack

I lay face down with my hands and feet tied to a
railroad track

I'm trapped and ain't nobody got my back

In a society that's built on everything except the
facts

I've felt pain so deep that I wanted to die

I've felt so much sorrow that I wanted to cry, but
couldn't, and I can't tell you why

Why are some so prejudiced?

Why is there so much violence?

Why is it that the real leaders somehow always get
silenced?

Nate Robinson

So many opinions circulate

But there's no way to debate

Because so few are open-minded to hear another
story

Only one could be true

Only one guess can satisfy you

If not, then we fight til one is black and blue

When nothin' can get solved if we fight each other

Yet so many hardheaded people exist that use
blindness as their cover

All these people make a brotha like me wanna kill
'em all until the only one left standin' is me

I've been hated on enough to drive the average
man insane

I wanna say a big "F" you, but then they've won the
game

The goal I have is to out-smart them

    And because of the love that's in my heart

To kill 'em with kindness then respark them

I'm layin' tracks on maps for what it's gonna take
for all of us to win

But if we can't put away our differences then our
future looks dim

    When are we gonna try to unify?

Because as time flies by we gettin' crazier

So many are caught up in they own lives and blind

That lovin' them isn't gettin' any easier

I ain't perfect I'm just spittin' Da Real

Tryin' to get this stuff off my chest and at the same
    time give you somethin' that you can feel

'Cause when we really look we all go through it

But we can't get along 'cause some fool always
    gotta know who you with?

Which side you on?

Like they done already past judgement

Havin' freedom is what's gonna make us all wanna
    pay our rent

Until then we all rollin' bodies that hold hundreds
    of dents

To me the truth is somethin' that we all can see

'Cause we was all born with it, but society's rules
    keep it hidden posted up stationary

Sometimes I wanna run through the streets
    screamin,' "F" the world"

'Cause it's this messed up stuff that's screwin' up
    the minds of too many young boys and girls

Please don't let go and hold on tight to life's never
    ending ride

    Only those that question will be answered

For if you don't question you've already died

                                    Nate Robinson

I'm dealin' with pressure

07/28/1999

I walk among the dead and don't even ask

When they see me on the street they just drive past

Thinkin' thoughts of indescribable feelins'

They run through my blood when I'm away from
the pad

Tryin' to stay away from da bad

Got me in the midst of finally breathin'

But as soon as I'm there everybody turns to
heathens

My mission is crystal clear

Get as far as I can away from here

I'm surrounded by people that would rather see me
gone

But who am I to judge them all because then I'm in
the wrong

I feel like it's the last chapter to a story that has no
end

But when I think about the stature I can barely
remember when it began

Am I a mouse in a maze used for experimentation?

Or does my life have meaning and all of this is just
preparation?

For only God knows and he's keepin' it a secret

Maybe I got information that I can only be discrete
    with

Tell me, am I walkin' down that narrow road where
    it's cold and only few travel?

My soul, couldn't possibly be sold

For this is my battle, my saddle

Tell me, who's gonna rattle the cages and who's
    gonna be the first to see the damage done?

    Or does the damage done to me prove more
    wounds?

Showing me that the war is almost won and the
    whole time I was the only one with the gun?

Scars, scratches, and teeth marks

Describe my mental state if you add street smarts

Who starts and gives out the invitations to this
    party?

I can see nothin' but torture ahead, but if that's
    what it takes to meet my goals then AMEN

I am not aware of too many teens as serious as me

    I understand tho

'Cause they can't see what I see

And they can't be who I'm gonna be

Just because I believe and am not completely
    deceived by what Satan's done to this whole
    planet

                                              Nate Robinson

I hate that sucka

He makes me wanna get off the topic, but he can't stop it

Because it was planned

From the get

I gotta think logic and not get washed away with him

Because in the end he's gonna get what he's gonna get

All I wish for everyone is the best

And that they would all show a little respect

To a brotha who's tryin' to do the right thing

So I'm strapped with God's vest

In case the devil wanna test

I ain't lyin' cause it says so in writing

My dream is in my ability

It's not just a possibility — anymore

So watch out for

What God's got in store for his child

Who grew up in a place where haters run wild

You might hate me, but I'm not gonna beat you with hatred

I'm gonna feed your soul with somethin' you couldn't possibly have already tasted

You've wasted almost your whole life til now

Because you had no clue and didn't know what to
    do with spiritual know-how

Or what it's all about

You need to open your mouth and let God fill it
    with knowledge and then some

I'm talkin' to myself too

So stick up your thumb and scream hallelujah

'Cause it's more than time to let God run through
    ya

                                    Nate Robinson

I believe he's got the answers

12/21/2000

I'm in the lowest depths of confusion

Can somebody feel my pain?

I try so hard to do right but end up doin' wrong
again

While caught up in life's struggles tryin' to figure
out what direction to choose

Understandin' if I pick the wrong one

Game over you lose

I'm goin' through a dry season in my spiritual walk

Can't worry about the reason that some mock the
talk

Walk the walk you talk

Don't talk the walk and get blocked

If you ain't got no "crunch time" brotha's on your
team you always gonna lose

No matter how good your jumper seems to be

The message is to get yourself clean

You don't have to do it yourself because you
can't

Give everything to him and he will make you gleam

No diamond ring or worldly thing can fill you like
Christ can

What can he bring me?

I don't have enough time to find out who is "he?"

Man, I'll never understand what makes the world
turn?

But how many gonna wait to find that answer and
take the time to learn?

Who am I to be the one to put anybody in their
place

How can I get across to people that this life is a race
of faith?

Whoever stands firm will be saved in the end

Some people been left on they own since they was
twelve and left alone to fend

Fend for themselves in this world of survival of the
richest

The ones who know the most are ones who live in
ditches

Trenches upon fences with barricades to block

Describe the defense system of so many because
they're too afraid to talk

To say what's real

To say what they truly feel

Is reality a fantasy or can it change?

Will I obtain what's been promised or will it remain
at an arm's length away?

Today I declare that Jesus Christ is Lord

                                        Nate Robinson

Tomorrow because of sorrow I lay in bed with a
　　whore

Who's to say what's right and what's wrong　　　　55

The word says the weak and the world says the
　　strong

I've decided that I'll just wait and see

　　Until that day even if I go astray

I'll put my trust in thee before I enter eternity

You feelin' me

My resurrection in my mental section

05/13/2000

As I sit here waitin' anticipatin' my blessin'

It got me guessin' and sometimes stressin'

But first I must learn the lesson

This verse is my suggestion

To my own ressurection in the mental section

As long as I stay caressin' the word the promises
are true

And they don't change to fit me or you

So what you gonna do when receivin' deceivin'
treatment?

From people you think are your friends

When in the end they can turn on you leavin' you
with no one to eat with

I was told to love them all

Regardless if they wanna see me fall or stand tall

I use his strength everyday to stay alive

I know this is for sure because there is no other
explanation to how I survive

Thoughtless acts and verbal words turned to guns
and spears

In my room I pray for strength and wisdom hopin'
somebody hears

Nate Robinson

Take away fear and beer and all that other type of
negative stuff

Around the corner every second the devil waits to
call it a bluff

Rough and rugged describe the true soldiers of the
living God

And not one of Satan's followers will be able to
escape the rod

Turn to his love

08/25/1999

How can I turn my back on him?

When all he's done for me is let me live

To breathe air and walk without any care

Is the best gift any of us could receive

I believe that there's more to life than what it
seems

    If we look real close than we will see

That his love covers us all over our body

And my heart, soul, and mind must be focused on
my dreams

I believe, every vision I have has been put in my
mind for me to achieve

And that every person I meet could've been put on
this earth to be a part of his team

I've got a passion for love and love got a passion for
me

If I just believe and apply than miracles from him
would fall from the sky

This ain't a lie

Everything I'm spittin' is real

'Cause it happened to me and his love I can feel

      Nate Robinson

Just because you can't see him doesn't mean he
    ain't around

It just means you need to open your heart and ears
    to hear his sound

His love is unconditional

Meaning that it never stops or quits

    Love like that you'll never find in a person

Unless he's involved, because like glue his love
    sticks and can take many hits

Take your pick before it's all over

I wanna serve the God of mercy

Not no politician whose only goal in life is to hurt
    me

Desert me when I need him/her the most

    A toast to the host

Who won't boast and wants to see all his children
    coast

But we need to mention

The devil who's in apprehension

At the moment you scared and runnin' in terror

From a God of love whose love and friendship is
    rare

Don't you care about anything or think bout
    eternity?

    'Cause I do and you need to

He's been here in the beginning of every century

I'm losin' my mind watchin' all you lost souls

You dead and don't even know it cause the devil
got a tight hold

This ain't about seein' who's the biggest "G"

He's tryin' to tell you and me

Forget everything you see and start lovin' me

If we stay blind for too long it will simply be too late

Because there's some people out here who just sit
around and wait, and anticipate his return

Where he will burn and turn everything to dust

I ain't offering a cake walk

Just help before you bust

You must not fall into the trap the devil's set

Even though we all have

You can bet that God still loves you and he won't let
go

And he wants to turn you into refined gold

                                    Nate Robinson

This ain't no cake walk

08/31/2002

What does it mean to win?

Why do we fight each other to win?

When winning has many different faces

How can one measure winning the journey of life?

Because it seems as though many judge their own
personal success based on what someone else
thinks

If you are different from the majority then you're
marked crazy or weird

The people that can withstand the constant
judgement and can still keep a good heart
toward others are strong people

Love eludes so many because so many are afraid to
truly commit to love

Because so many are afraid of the vulnerability that
love warrants from its partaker

Have you ever loved before?

Has love ever hurt you before?

Your heart must taste defeat before you can truly
enjoy success

People's selfishness makes it hard for them to see
what true strength is

Because true strength comes from within the soul
of a person

It's not boastful or proud

It doesn't need to prove itself to anyone

It doesn't seek fame or notoriety

True strength lies within the boundaries of true
humility

But to have true humility one must experience pain
and turmoil

One must taste death

Death to self

And going through dying is a process of excruciating
pain that seems to never stop

A person is met with one challenge to overcome
followed by another and another

But this is the marking of a true Christian

For the one that survives he/she will be given the
crown of grace

Which God has promised to those that love him

To love God with all your heart, for this is truly the
only duty of man

Can you love your neighbor as yourself?

Would you give your life for someone you don't
know?

Are you truly happy?

                                    Nate Robinson

Or do you put on the front, but secretly you sit in
the pool of despair?

The real answer to every important question has
something to do with God

Some might deny it or try to find a way around it,
but no matter which way you slice it it's true

Why do we hang on to things and people that
will not give us any leverage on the day of
judgement?

Is it because we fear what others might say or
think?

Is it because we fear the naked feeling of individual
isolation?

If we break fear than we overcome

But to overcome one must go through the
unavoidable valley of dying to the flesh

And that journey can take months, years, and
maybe even decades

But to reach the top of that hill on the other side of
the valley

The top of that hill is the resting place of the very
cross that Jesus died on for each one of us

To reach that place is to become forever changed
into becoming a whole and complete human
being

It is to find out who you really are in Christ Jesus

It is to simply die for

But how many are willing to pay the price?

For the road that leads to salvation is narrow and
    only few find it

In other words,

The road that leads you through the valley is hard
    to find and few will even see it let alone finish its
    course

Are you willing to pay the price?

Because you will lose friends

Because you will go through stress and drama

Because you will die

But you will be purfied and come out as pure gold
    when and if you reach the top of that hill

For those who seek to save their lives will lose
    them

But those who lose their lives for his sake will find
    true life

ARE YOU WILLING TO DIE?

                                    Nate Robinson

Principles I can't forget

06/21/2000

What is it about God that makes our hopes come alive?

What is it about eternal life that makes it easy to survive?

Revive what's been broken to pieces

Jesus ain't no thesis

Just ask the deceased

At least just give him a chance

Against the fear of losin' everything and watchin' time pass

What if I run out of gas and how long will it last?

During your test is when you arise to the task

With the help of a beloved father

Who strengthens our faith with patience and endurance

We are sure to finish the race somehow

Read the bible if you need reassurance

This occurance will test

And after feel blessed

For he punishes those he loves

Whether born in rags or riches look for this from above

In love he deals

With all those who are real

And those who are fake

    He pushes all the right buttons

    Just in the nick of time

So fear not for you will not break

Just take a time out of any situation that's thick

With God on your side

Tell me can any enemy ride?

So ain't no need to hide behind pride

A new man has been created and the old one just
   died

The devil lied when he said you've already tried

In order to keep your will tied up and led astray

So tell him in Jesus name

That the games that once were played are over

For I have found a better way and stand firm when
   I proclaim

That the devil is a liar

God's gonna take me higher

Higher than I've ever been

Knowin' that's it's sink or swim

I take my chances knowin' the truth

Better late than never

Like my next door neighbor's Pops

But take advantage while you still a youth

And that's the truth

Why?

I don't know

And maybe I'll never know what's goin' on?

One things for sure, I'm gonna spend life doin' right
    from wrong

Humility

07/13/2000

I'm in no hurry or rush

Because of the fact that I love you so much

Love for you is shown by following your commands

I want to try my best to accept your helping hands

Every time I'm down you pick me up

When I surrender at your feet you fill my cup

You're not interested in details you give it to me
    straightforward

Help me to be humble and wise

And to cut off every urge to put on any disguise

No need to size the competition cause there is
    none

    My faith decrees he's got a plan for us all

No need to run

What we need is patience and endurance

Combined with our love for him eternity's our
    assurance

I'm askin' for whatever you want to give

Who am I to give demands to the one who enables
    me to live?

                    Nate Robinson

Message to the body of Christ

08/24/2000

There's a deeper level of intimacy to be reached

A lot deeper than we can humanly see

I believe God's callin' us to even touch his face and
lips

And challengin' us to search his word for tips

When the desire to straight serve him with
everything is placed in our hearts

Then and only then will we see a great move of
God start

All these pastor's is preachin' but does the body get
it?

We need to be able to feed ourselves yet somehow
we forget

We are blessed because we serve a merciful God

"I desire mercy, not sacrifice."

Is what saves us all from the rod

We'd be goin' to hell if it weren't for Christ

The more you know the more you grow

Which enables God to enhance your sight

Be ready for a fight

Each and every single night

Because the devil's words are smart, not dumb

How can we win the race if we're too afraid and
    won't even run?

It's fun to truly know and communicate with God

It's unfathomable to know that in heaven he's
    reserving a spot

For you

For you and only you

Trust in the Lord with all your heart and lean not on
    your own understanding

Acknowledge him in all your ways and he shall
    direct your paths

Recitin' verses like these is how we kill the enemy
    before he has a chance to mess with us

We'd rather sit back and get beat up while our
    bodies rust and turn to dust

But wait, I'm tired of things just stayin' the same

I've gotta start standin' on the word

Sayin' that all things work to the good for those
    that love him in Jesus name

I claim my salvation and am under construction

For he that began a good work in me shall finish it
    until the end of the world

Through my consistent submission

It's the devil's butt that I'm kickin' and God's lips
    that I'm kissin'

No more past and reminiscin'

                                    Nate Robinson

Just future plans and promises from he that lives
    above

    Not being' scared when I mess-up

Cause even then all he wants is a hug

I accept the love that you give

And know and believe servin' God is the only way
    to live

The Blueprint

08/31/2000

How can you describe what God is doing?

If you've given your life to him

You've put your faith and your trust in him

Everything you dream of is riding on him

First, understand he longs to know you

"Depart from me you workers of iniquity, I never
  knew you."

To live with him we must die

We must hmble ourselves before we can fly

Worship God in spirit and in truth

Meanin' be honest with him in everything you do

Hold on for the ride is bumpy

You won't know where you are going until he
  reveals where he's taking you

Those that truly have done what God has called
  them to do have died to their flesh

In order to past their prepared test

Love the Lord your God with all of your heart, mind,
  and soul

Would mean that all of your attention would be
  focused on him

Then he says,

Nate Robinson

Love your neighbor as yourself. Giving you
    direction

No secret code or detection is needed

In our case just the blood to be pleaded

And the word to be feeded to your souls

Let the God of love take complete control

I'm on a roll

Tryin' to maintain as I stroll through biblical
    principles that I am learnin'

To win the war with the devil it's gonna take some
    discernin'

While always turnin' the way God would have you
    turn

Without the peace of God it's a guranteed crash
    and burn

You learn to discern with Gods' perfect trainin' and
    perseverance

    You out-smart your enemy knowin' you have
    authority

With the blood of Christ as your assurance

To combine right standin' preachin' and teachin' oh
    what a powerful thing

    To combine applyin' the word, praise, and prayer
    to a God fearin' life

Represents what gives the devil a sting

And what brings glory and honor to an Almighty
    King

And what can keep your flesh and spirit clean,
    know what I mean

74

                    Nate Robinson

I want out

09/14/2000

Change my thoughts, my life from the inside out

    While I'm holdin' on to you in faith

And tryin' not to doubt

I'm not perfect as you well know

But I'm determined to stay real and not get caught
    up in a show

I flow freely when fresh out of the throne room

More of you is my desire I won't except my spiritual
    doom

Cause the devil loom around seekin' whom he may
    destroy

Through my submission to God, patience, and
    perseverance, I will gain eternal life at a price

Mixed with endurance and Gods' courage

The door to our spiritual freedom is openin' and
    closin' everyday

But you gotta go through the one who said, "I am
    the truth, the light, and the way."

For the only way to the Father is through the Son

Many of us choose the road to destruction and
    don't even know it

But we will find out when we look up in the twinkle
    of an eye and see Jesus comin' in his father's
    glory

    Claimin' we want to change but it's too late
    because it's judgment day,

And you can't change your life's story

That's why we need to take a serious look at what's
    underneath

And allow God to change our hearts before we
    can't breathe

No deed can get you in

Because Jesus was willin' to bleed to cover your sin

To end the power of darkness over every man

Enablin' man to take a stand with power and
    authority in his name

For forgiveness of sin and to show us how to live is
    why he came

You all besta believe he's comin' again

    To redeem those who chose to follow

And to rid the new world of sin

Then the real fun begins

What I'm sayin' is without Jesus there's no way
    around it, you just can't win livin' a life of sin

                                    Nate Robinson

Gotta get rid of pride

10/01/2000

You're gonna serve somethin' you were created to

So put your trust in Christ instead of what you do

For you were saved by grace not by your works

This life is nothin'

You were born from and when you die you'll return
to dirt

Don't skirt and mess up your spiritual growth spurt

Instead turn to Jesus and let his blood take away
the hurt

His love is the most powerful thing alive

With sellin' your soul to the devil you're guaranteed
to take a dive

Don't stand up in my face and lie and pretend you
got it all together

God knows you go home and cry

Without Christ you're sure to die and burn in hell's
fire forever

That's why I'm intense when I speak

Understandin' he's strong when I'm weak

Seek and you will find

Knock and the door will be opened for you

Don't live a lie anymore God can deliver you from
    whatever it is you've been through

I'm learnin' who God really is

He's the creator of all this and smarter than any
    math wiz

Can pass any pop quiz

I don't care what your problem is — HE'S GREATER

Don't be a hater and act proud

Accept his gift of redemption and do away with
    your doubt

I don't know about you, but I'm livin' for Christ

Without thinkin' twice

I'm acceptin' his blood and livin' with his promise of
    eternal life, alright

                              Nate Robinson

My inner perception

01/03/2001

I remain the joker in your deck of cards

    Hated on by many, but still here

Ah man, life is hard

I look around my surroundings and right now

I believe that love exist for me still somehow

Girl, wipe that sad look off your face

And come receive a hug from a brotha with a warm
embrace

What is this place that we livin' in?

And somebody needs to explain why is it that we
sin and fight to win?

The bible says that we wrestle not against flesh and
blood

Only those who read can understand this loaded
stud

When you speak it every demon in hell ears is
plugged

What is it gonna take to see negativity drug through
the mud?

I say that true love is worth fightin' for

And the truth is what I'm waitin' for

As I'm bypassin' many females to wait for my one

Although I sometimes slip I still believe that she'll
    come

Findin' my purpose is what sums up my whole case

If you still don't get it, try this, who is Nate?

Goin' deeper into the heart of a human

Seein' scars and bruises from other people who
    pursued him

Never quite could understand why he was the way
    he was

Lookin' in the mirror askin' how did you become?

The person that stared back looked confused when
    he said

    All you can do is have faith and thank God that
    you're not dead

Holdin' back tears from wounded moments in my
    life

Has left me feelin' alone and empty while I search
    to find the light

But what light?

Can't you see, I'm in the middle of a circle of other
    people's suggestions

Who's to say who's right and who's wrong is my
    question?

We are all entitled to our own opinion

Got too many people lettin' other people take over
    their dominion

                                      Nate Robinson

Personally, I could care less but it's stress dealin'
    with some people

'Cause the truth is all people are not treated equal

It doesn't have to just be about your race

People now-a-days use anything like how pretty is
    your face?

The question is do you have enough strength not to
    fight back?

The fact is it's harder to take it and easier to fight
    back

Life has many lessons available to those willing to
    learn

No matter how far you get you'll never be able to
    change the way this world turns

How much you earn only determines your physical
    state

And haven't we learned money isn't everything all
    it takes is one earthquake

To separate you from you money

You from your honey

Then everything you made has amounted to not

You thought you were invisible now look what you
    got

Pride comes before the fall

Yet we all seem to have to hit rock bottom before
    we want to answer that call

Holdin' on to useless things I'm talkin' to myself too

'Cause ain't no tellin' what life brings just ask the
    guy in the fatal car wreck to come and talk to
    you

Worried about your rings it seems to me you tryin'
    to fill a void

It's a void that no earthly thing can fill are we still
    learning?

Now this is the place where I drop you off

Because this is where my life is right now, at least a
    glimpse

Ooh watch the curb I meant to talk soft

Nate Robinson

This mental parole

01/30/2001

I rolled up my sleeves it's time to do the dirty work

Down in the dirt where ain't nothin' else but hurt

Some brotha's make it and some brotha's don't

    The ones too afraid to question

Those brotha's won't

You can bet I'm walkin' through hot coals

Hot coals of charcoal

The fire feels like it's eatin' through my bones

In the end I'm supposed to sparkle

Imagine walkin' a tight rope thirty stories above
    ground

Everybody is holdin' they breath cause you fall if
    they make a sound

The only thing you can focus on is something you
    cannot see

It's the voice of a loving father calling softly, "Come
    to me."

Imagine inner-woven lines of poetry

Captured on the fingertips of this brotha outside of
    a computer screen showin' me

Blowin' me away with the thoughts in his heart

All he ever wanted really was to be understood

Felt ashamed over something he had no control
over cause he wasn't from the hood

Fell in love with the art of music and the expression
of the soul

Realized what people really needed is true freedom
so they could escape this mental parole - that
we all face

'Cause every person wants to know why we run the
race?

Some people believe this and some people believe
that

But will enough evidence ever be presented to
make one belief fact?

Faith and hope says yes reality says no

I choose hope cause hope is what wakes us up
every morning

Without it we'd all be completely dead robots and
dormant

But wait most have already lost they hope

We need to come up with a solution to regain
what's been stole

God when they read this please take complete
control and set us all free from this mental
parole

                                        Nate Robinson

The path we must take

03/30/2001

Now is the time for the ultimate unification

A unification that will shake this whole nation

No one man can do it all alone

It's gonna take complete submission to the one
    that's on the throne

Tell me, what can stop a body of people willing to
    stick together?

Together forever, no matter what tries to rip the
    chain apart

We're dealin' with matters of the heart

Take a journey - a journey that frees a man's soul

Beware because your enemies will stop at nothing
    to seize all control

When you stay on the right path - nothing can stop
    you

    Because all possible distractions

    That cause negative reactions

Have nothin' to cling to

What you need to remember is this path is not
    beauty

    It contains thistles and thorns

And not much description for your purpose and
    duty

So if the night time shadows begin to crowd your
    space

Causin' you to fear this path's cold embrace

Gather yourself, cause the pain is only temporary

The brotha's that don't make it are the same ones
    that couldn't carry

Relay this message to your brain - that it's kinda
    scary

And the only way to win is to never stop walkin'

Realizin' that no matter what you do - some people
    will never stop talkin'

There will be doubters along the way

People that hate and people that sway away

Allowin' themselves to be influenced by outside
    suggestions

But always know that nothin' in history has topped
    Jesus' resurrection

If questions arise, don't trip cause it's only normal

Ain't no rule in life that says everything you do
    must be formal

And if ever attacked by an unseen creature

    Just sit back - relax

'Cause with God on your side they know they could
    never defeat ya

          Nate Robinson

Unify, we must unify

'Cause if we don't try - we are guaranteed to die

This ain't no lie - knowin' this, you can never deny

If we don't fly - then we fry

More people need to be askin' the question, why?

'Cause if we don't try to unify

Then more and more evil will soon arise

So you can't be surprised with the situation we
    now face

    Because we tried to fight with muscle

When all it took was faith

Take a look at hate and fate

Then ask yourself if you alone have what it takes to
    break?

What makes us great is not fightin' crime like a
    superhero would

    But doin' your part and workin' together

To help create what can make this country good

If you would - you could - you should - no excuses

Life's lessons

04/01/2001

I write poetry to express what's on my chest

I can say that writin' puts my thoughts to text

I rest when in front of this computer screen

Life's tests force me to use writin' words as a means
of mental survival

'Cause sometimes I feel suicidal

And I can't decide whether it'd be better to live or
die

The world around me don't change and won't
change

Because it's set up this way

What's worse is the people on top can look me in
the eye and try to tell me that I have an honest
say

But what they can do is throw that BS away

Because I'm facin' stress each and every single day

Because of the games they play

They got us workin' they jobs to eat

Secretly we slaves

But few can feel the shackles on they feet

You so busy that you don't even notice

They got you thinkin' you winnin' they game

                                        Nate Robinson

When really you just a novice

You playin' a game that was designed to make you
    lose

They've been weedin' us out since grade school

So they'd know who to choose

Who would obey every word they say

Who wouldn't ask questions when they say

    "You suppose to dress this way"

    "Talk this way and walk this way"

And if you don't join today then you can go live in
    the ghetto

We've been lied to since day one

When they told you that "image is everything"

'Cause only when you on top - they come

And when you on the bottom - they run

And laugh at you - for they fun

Here's a word from the wise - that they's dumb

The solution to our problems is to find inner peace

'Cause you can have all the money in the world, but
    still have no peace

We must learn to reach down deep inside our souls

So we can teach others how to break society's
    powerful hold

It's cold the way it is, but it's the truth

How many people is dyin' and still a youth?

How many people is tryin' only to find out that they
was born to lose?

Then you can watch their desire slowly fade away

'Cause very few are resilient

Just goin' to school don't make you brilliant

Havin' peace in your heart is the only way to go

But society's got this distorted

'Cause you can look good, but havin' no peace in
your heart is somethin' you just can't ignore

Learn to explore your possibilities

'Cause ain't no right or wrong way to get to know
yourself

The Bible says that you must first take the plank out
of your own eye before you can help anybody
else

So understand that the purpose of your existence
cannot be served

If you steady stay on the corna - perved and on the
curb

Because you as an individual are worth more

Why not turn to your creator to ask for help to
explore?

Don't ignore the fact that we all have something to
offer

The problem is we've all been brainwashed and
think it's better to be hard than softer

                                          Nate Robinson

Towards people that could end up to be the
     greatest asset to your life

But some think that you gotta be hard to be tight

That ain't right

For some it fits, but not for all

You can't allow fear to stop you from reachin' your
     full potential

Bein' yourself is cool enough

For all those that say it ain't - I'm callin' your bluff

'Cause some would rather be rough and some
     prefer to play the role

But there's somethin' in the atmosphere that says
     there's a medium

And it lies within havin' self control

When you better yourself - you better those around
     you

When you lose all control - anger and hate will
     surely surround you

So take heed to these words and learn to love

     And rid yourself of pride

'Cause it's the man up above that holds your plug

Cut the rope

03/26/2001

I've seen a lot, but what does it all amount to?

Some people now know my name

When fame was never somethin' that a brotha
sought after

Now tamed and out the game my mentality has
changed

But questions remain the same in my brain

The information that was gained has put a strain on
the way that I now see thangs

It's kinda strange livin' with very little hope

And at the same time strugglin' cause it seems
impossible to cut the rope

That hangs around a brotha's neck

Although it was fitted to choke me

    Still I breathe - as I wheeze

    Because my Mama's on her knees - as she
    pleads

The longer I live the stronger I get

The more they try and kill me the more I won't quit

The battle I face lies within my mind

I feel like I'm runnin' a race with no finish line

Nate Robinson

I can decide to conform to the options that society gave me

But I'd rather die than let another man dictate Nate

So I wait like Joseph did in the Old Testament

I was told through prophecy that my destiny is heaven sent

Not to remain a resident in this mental holdin' cell

Or to refrain from followin' my dreams only to fail

I'm goin' through spritually organized trainin' to become a true warrior

'Cause when this gift from God speaks - Not I but the Holy Spirit takes over

With powerful words that leave scars and require medical treatment to heal

In order that many can be saved and know the truth

So more people can be real and feel inner peace

Instead of searchin' on every corna for somethin' that's rare on the streets

Ain't no Police gonna stop this movement

What's written in the Bible shall not return void

It's already started by takin' your hemroids away

Forget what them doubters say

You can change today

I suggest that you do it right away

Before it's too late and you stand before the
  Creator of all things

Cause there's no way that we all came from
  monkeys

You gotta get one thing straight

There's no time to debate about if he's real or if
  he's fake

Because what's on the line is your eternal existence

Before you decide ask yourself,

What's gonna be the verdict and your eternal life's
  sentence?

Cut the rope

                                          Nate Robinson

We are working for our eternal existence

04/09/2001

I feel as though I'm beggin' to see above the
surface

I've been underground so long searchin' for my
purpose

I'm conscious of the fact that happiness comes and
goes

But I'ma try to hold on to each blessin' I receive -
this I know

I'm gonna end up wherever God puts me

'Cause it's not I that can change my situation, but
his Holy Spirit workin' through me

I used to be blinded by my own guidance because I
couldn't see

That I had to step back and allow him to put the
right situations in front of me

Then simply do what it takes to finish what's on my
plate

And the whole time I've been being molded into
the Nate he wanted to create

My fate is still a complex matter

I'm dealin' with stress while I'm climbin' life's
ladder

I gotta voice and I gotta choice to proclaim the
    name that's hookin' me up

  Lookin' me up and he's shakin' me up

  'Cause he's takin' me up while he's bakin' me up

I'm in the womb of destiny chillin'

I ain't trippin' cause he said he made me who I am
    before my birth

Before the creation of his green and blue earth

And I'm worth the price of a kings' son

The games gotta be played even though I've already
    won

He's never done and I could be a bum

And still be used to help someone else to see his
    kingdom come

This is not for fun

'Cause to see his kingdom come - you can't play
    dumb

But gotta know his son and cherish 'em

Because what he did is what enables us all to run

And no I'm not done

Because we haven't seen his son yet

You can bet before it's over enemy lines will be
    wrecked and checked

Put in they place for steppin' to his face

Understand he don't fight with weapons he fights
    with grace

                                          Nate Robinson

And he's never in your face

He just gives his love and then gives you the choice
and the opportunity to embrace

Because when it's all over we all gonna have to
fight a case

One in which we have no say

No power to exploit and money to persaude the
judge

Because we only get one chance

One chance to live - one chance to breathe

Once chance to give - one chance to belive

Then it's over

And when it's over ain't no turnin' back

How long can you hold your breath under fire and
torture?

Before I leave ask yourself that

Soul search

08/25/2001

A thin slice of heaven is what we all is chasin'

With this world livin' fast pace it's hard to stay
patient

While being presented with all sorts of pathways to
choose from

Then when you finally come to your conclusion

It seems that someone's always there to call your
solution dumb

I come to the forefront a soldier

With this weight of time weighin' down on my
shoulders

So many of us are gettin' colder and colder

While the problems we all face are gettin older and
older

What is it gonna take to shake the fakeness that we
all see?

I hope and pray to God that he would use me

'Cause through my observations ain't too many
people on earth that are truly free

We work so hard to cover up all of our faults

When God's not judgin' us like people are

Yet still we refuse to give him the combination to
our inner vaults

                                          Nate Robinson

I wanna see people real and open

    Honest to themselves and others

Instead of always complainin' puttin' on a front and mopin'

We pass judgment down on others as many times as we take a shower

And somewhere in the middle of all this we forgot about who really has the power

It's easier to hate than it is to love

It's easier to give up or give in than it is to try or to challenge

Why settle for being a sheep led to slaughter?

When all that you seek can be found if you are wiling to work that much harder

Be willing to try and fail but expect success

'Cause as long as you've put all your faith in him - expect nothing less than the best

It's time to stop caring or thinking about what other people think

    And learn to love yourself for you

'Cause when that happens your eyes are truly open to blink

There's no question there's a lot of messed up things in the world and it seems there's so little you can do

But when you begin to think that way

Just remember that you were once in sin and God
left the ninety-nine on the hill just to save you

                                    Nate Robinson

My survival

01/23/2003

To survive - to live - to experience life

To live free of fear - free of doubt

What can they do to stop what can't be stopped?

Just watch as what was destined to be is fulfilled
through the blessings that come down from
heaven

What can you do?

What can you do?

Don't stop - don't quit - never give up

If you have to crawl

If you have to drag yourself through the mud -
through the gravel - don't stop

Just believe that nothing that is done in his name is
done in vain

What can they do?

Watch him work through me

Because I believed that anything was possible

I believed that he would do what he said he could
do

All you non-believers will believe

What can they do to stop what can't be stopped?

Like a train coming full speed towards anything in
    its path

Destiny is going to win no matter what it takes

Lean not on your own understanding

His thoughts and his ways are above my ways - they
    are above your ways

What can they do?

Watch - just watch

The day is coming closer and closer

Years and years of struggle

The gift to overcome adversity

The strength to endure anything

What can they do that they haven't tried to do
    already?

They can try to hate

They can try to make fun of me

They can call me names

They can try to fight me

They can try anything they want to, but I will not
    fall

I might look like I am going to fall, but I will not fall
    down

I will never give up - I will never quit - I will never
    die

Because he is with me - because he is inside of me -
    because he is my every breath

                                    Nate Robinson

What can they do?

What can they do?

What can they do to stop me?

I am with him until the day I die

Until my last breath

He has a plan

It hurts sometimes, but I am better for it

He's taught me about what is important in life

About what it takes to win

It takes faith

Can you believe in what you can't see?

Can you believe that he will give you what he told
you he would give when you can't see what he's
gonna do or how he's going to do it?

Can you believe?

Hold on for dear life

True people go through the fire

Because we all are going to go through the fire

You cannot avoid it

But how are you going to go through it?

Survive - survive by any means necessary

I will not die - I refuse to die

I have been through so much crap that I can't even
describe the stuff to myself

I have wanted to die night after night

I have wanted to die

I have wanted to die

To stop my breathing

Get this crap over with

I'm going to die sooner or later - why not now?

I'm in the dark and I can't see

No one cares about what happens to me

Everybody else has their own problems to deal with

Who cares about happens to me?

No one, but the one who died for me when I was
    not even born yet

No one, but the one who controls and who made
    the universe

No one, but the one who has been there for me the
    whole time

He told me that he would never leave me nor
    forsake me - but I didn't believe him

He told me that he would leave ninety-nine just to
    save me - but I didn't believe him

He told me that all things are possible to those that
    dare to believe in him - but I didn't believe him

So he showed me that he was there for me

He showed me that he cared for me - that he loved
    me unconditionally

Because I spit in his face everyday - but he still
    blessed me

                                    Nate Robinson

Because I cursed him - but he still blessed me

Because I gave up - but when I was faithless he was
faithful

Because he has always been there for me

Because he has always loved me

That's why I trust him with my life now

That's why he is in control of the steering wheel
now

That's why I believe him when he tells me that all of
this is happening for a reason

That's why

That's why

What can they do?

What can they do?

You don't have to believe, but I will

You don't have to think that he is in complete
control of what is happening on earth everyday,
but I will

You don't have to praise him for your life, but I will

I will

I will

And what can they do to stop what can't be
stopped?

Destiny is going to take place in my life

And I going to be used in a mighty way wreck the
devils plans

And what can he do?

What can he do to stop what can't be stopped?

What can't be stopped is God - God in me

Dedicated to all you haters

You can't beat him so join him

You can't hate him because he loves you regardless

So why fight his love when you could just sit back
and enjoy it

This ain't no cake walk and it took me going
through hell to begin to understand the love he
has for me

He loves me so much that he would discipline me
to build my character

I didn't understand then and I barely understand
now, but it's God

It's God

It's God

What can he do?

It's God

                                    Nate Robinson

Chapter Three

Questions

Enter by the narrow gate; for wide is the gate and broad is the way that leads to destruction, and there are many who go in by it. Because narrow is the gate and difficult is the way which leads to life, and there are few who find it.

Matthew 7: 13-14

Wuz da deal

Wuz da deal with all these phonies tryin' to claim
   real

Give me somethin' I can feel

Because of my sometimes fading will

I'd kill facts and tactics

Used by those who I refer to as the actress

My mattress, once a waterbed

With fatal blows to my head

A more mature state of mind and thinking

That won't rot

With God, I could never be caught or sought out

Sometimes forgot I mount and count my blessings

While stressing - leaving many of peoples guessing
   with the person I present

Represent - but represent what?

No more fronts with stunts designed to cover over
   one's eyes

Don't play the wise guy with your disguise and lies
   - why?

           Nate Robinson

Why is it?

Why is it that bustas' gotta have a problem with
   me?

Always tryin' to imitate what they see on TV

Why is it that my life had to turn out this way?

   Forcin' patience on my part

Makin' me wait for my day

Why is it that friends can't stay real with each
   other?

And everywhere you go everybody's trippin' over
   color

Discover what seems to be missing

Then maybe we could end all this dissing

Why is it that to get somewhere you have to suffer?

And now-a-days people act dumber and dumber

Why do I feel the way I do inside?

I wish I could fly freely

A place where everyone around could see me
   happy and free

Free of all this situational stress

A place where my mind could be at rest

No test - no lust

Just success without rust

Why is it that I'm still alive?

And when will he tell me that it's my time to arise?

To be the young man he called me to be

Mark the date when all the prisoners are set free

Why is it that I have the urge to write?

Why is it that I want to stay up every night?

Why is it that some of my questions have no
    answer?

                                    Nate Robinson

Break free

07/24/2000

What separates the human race but fate?

What will it take to break my faith?

Some are under the influence of pressure and
stress

Others live it up, yet fight for who's best

Very few can see that this life is a test

Scientist would rather resort to an uneducated
guess

If we could all feel each other, then what would
happen?

All hate and fear would be lost and we could
receive his peace

How could you tell someone who has been through
hell that Jesus loves them?

And expect them to understand and believe that
their life's gonna get any better

When they've been doin' hard labor for thirty years

How many tears do we let go unwiped?

Because we just think of ourselves when we go to
bed every night

If we were really concerned with the world around
us

Enough to go out of our way to help those in need

Then and only then would we be doin' what Jesus
    did as an everyday routine

Free your mind and the rest will follow

Let the devil have your spirit and watch your heart
    turn hollow

Analyzing what I've seen

Hoping that my eyes and heart always stay keen

Prayin' to God and expectin' answers has led me to
    this conclusion

To do something of tremedous worth you must be
    led by the spirit

    Until that day I wait patiently

Doin' work and seekin' his face in order to hear it

                                    Nate Robinson

Amazing Grace

06/23/2000

When dreams fade and faith is all that remains -
  what can you do?

Look and seek diligently for a Savior who longs to
  know you

Easier said than done as I am finding out for myself

The thing is most peoples dreams somehow involve
  getting wealth

Not health or the kingdom

Unfortunately it's all about self

I wanna change all that mess

But feelings sometimes overwhelm and overpower
  me

I need the sin cleasin' blood to break the shackles
  off my feet

So we finally meet - me and Jesus that is

He wants to wash me clean

He wants to give me everything I desire

He wants the Holy Spirit to baptize me with fire

Take me higher and let me see clear

First, he says, "You must give away what you hold
  dear."

"For he who wants follow me must take up his
cross."

"And he who seeks to save his life will end up
beaten and lost."

Disappointed and confused I struggled to look at
his face

He looked at me smiled and said, "Let me tell you
about my fathers **AMAZING GRACE.**"

                                    Nate Robinson

No turnin' back

07/14/2000

I am so glad that I have you to fall back on

No matter what I face or whatever could go wrong

In many times of need you remain strong

Day-after-day and year-after-year

The more I grow in you the more I see clear

You open both ears to hear

Please, draw me near

Because I have the utmost fear and respect for you

Make me a mirror that enables you to shine
through

Do whatever it takes

Let my final product take the shape of that of Christ

Help me to pray in the spirit and please open my
spiritual sight

Let me loose to fight

As soon as my spiritual man has built up enough
might

Stronger and stronger I grow

I love you Lord and realize that there is never
enough to be absorbed from your knowledge
and love

I beg at your feet

To be used in a unique productive type of way

No matter what they say

I have decided not to be led astray

I don't care what I have to pay

Because I am unconditionally loved

By the Creator of earth and all that lies above

I have decided to follow Jesus no turnin' back

I have picked up my cross denied myself and
    allowed him to pick up my slack

Nate Robinson

Chaos in my brain

08/03/2000

One question

Where will you be when all my desire fades to
  serve thee?

I feel like hangin' it up and callin' it quits

Lettin' the boss know that today I'm sick

Lord I can't help but be real

I can't escape how I feel

I'm lookin' at all these pastors, evangelists,
  speakers, and how they speak and preach of you

I'm lookin' at myself thinkin' how could I be used by
  you?

What's it gonna take to see me through?

All this garbage that I hold inside

All this frustration that I just can't hide

Sometimes I think I'd rather die than stay alive

Facin' every different routine I find myself in

Hopin' and prayin' one day it'll all end

Whose my true friend?

I think of one, but it's the complete opposite of
  what I wanted

I'm worried about worldly things

Like, what would they think and what's this gonna
    do to my image?

Religion, is something I see more and more

So because I'm different does that mean I'm goin'
    the right way?

The way I view each day or what I refer to as play

Every single word I say

What does it all add up to?

Man, sometimes I just feel blue

Caught and drug down by the world around you

I'm sick of this I'm supposed to have power and if I
    don't then I'm just lost

Just to see who's boss

Jesus paid the cost

Because we all were lost

And if he'd leave ninety-nine to save one then what
    does that say about the true boss?

How much he cares and shares with us

Yet, we put the hammer down

What ever happened to love?

What ever happened to it?

Tell me what have all of us become?

God I need you

You know the cry of my heart

Please oh please let me be used as a spark

                              Nate Robinson

In the dark when will my circumstances change?

How much longer do I have to stand in the rain and feel internal pain?

Teach me to love like Dain

I don't want to be playin' with you or anybody else

If we could have a little unity than maybe we could get somewhere

Instead of a different church every block

How much more power if we joined as one?

If we were really committed to each other and let God be number one

This is for fun - I'm done

Patiently/impatiently waiting

10/09/2000

Lord, I need your help to get me through

I need your spirit to enable me to do what I've been
    called to do

I'm feelin' set back and held down

I'm tryin' hard not to frown

Despite the fact that they clown

I'm still down for you

No matter what you take me through

Because you are what is truth

What needs to be taught to our youth

I'm takin' sucka punches in the mouth and done
    lost some of my teeth

Hurtin' on the inside, but feedin' off every time we
    meet

Holdin' on strong to your words

You use what the world labels foolish to confound
    the wise

Meanin' I just gotta take everything and think, "In
    due time"

Humble myself to be exalted

Even though I sometimes feel as if I've lost it

The cost is high

                                          Nate Robinson

Don't have time to ask why

'Cause I believe I can fly through Christ who strengthens me

While devastated I have peace

While broken and hurting because of faith the pain will cease

At least I'm goin' to heaven

'Cause my redemption is fact not feelin'

What's the message?

Don't give up and dare to believe

The more you humble yourself the more you open yourself up to receive

For he corrects those he loves

My correction is divine and comes from above

Soft as a dove, yet wise as snakes

The more God is in me the more I can take before I break

Is it too late?

My life is in your hands

10/31/2000

My mind tries to fight it, but I have decided

That my life is in your hands

Lord my life is filled with questions

Let alone other peoples suggestions

On how to serve you and how to stay true

Even when I feel blue and confused with the way
things are goin' in my life

And every other day I feel like I'm ridin' on a
freakin' roller coaster ride

With you alongside there's no reason to hide

Sometimes strugglin' with pride and acceptin' the
devil's lies

Leads to a compromise in my faith

I try not to hesitate or debate

That you can take nothin' and make somethin' out
of ones' faith

But it's my trustin' that I need you to elevate

I wanna be real not fake

And wanna take your word for what it says by
exceptin' your grace

We da ones that make your gospel complex

I wanna believe that, "Greater is he …….. "

 Nate Robinson

So I can pass every test

And every step I want to be ordered of the Lord

For faith credits righteousness in the sight of God
    when readin' Romans chapter four

Lord please open the door so I can soar like the
    eagle

I wanna be used for your purposes and for your
    glory

In order to help people see the real story

But first I must learn for myself

For I too am in need of your help

A state of confusion

12/13/2000

I'm at a vulnerable state in my faith

I've seen signs and evidence that I can not debate

Enough to make anyone who says God isn't real a
fake

How can a man have a relationship with something
he can not see?

It's that simple question that makes it hard for me

I wanna be free, but what is freedom?

It changes with each persons definition

Knowin' I'm saved is it fact or fiction?

This friction that continually haunts my well being

Can be blamed on an evil spirit according to my
faith that's steamed

He's hot because God relentlessly keeps pursuing
me

And even when I mess up I still long to be free

Reality and life - how do they combine?

Through complete submission and faith is how you
let your light shine

There's a fine line between good and evil

How can one spirit inhabit in and love all people?

Controlling what we can not see

                                    Nate Robinson

Holding the key to each person's destiny

Imagination and contemplation coupled with
    exaggeration and pure frustration is enough to
    drive anybody crazy

Believin' that what keeps me sane is the one that
    made me

He gave me a mom that's like any others

A very unique individual is what I have discovered

Why was I placed in the situation I'm in?

And will I someday be able to call my wife my best
    friend?

Is it a sin to want to know the truth?

    By being open minded

Feelin' like your being blinded and always being
    reminded that the triangle of life is obtuse

Is there a such thing as mental abuse?

Am I putting what I've been given to proper use?

I'm runnin' out of time

What path do I choose?

Did I lose?

Blind faith

01/04/2001

This is torture, torture not being able to express the
    way I feel completely

Lately, aside from the fact that I don't understand
    why God made me

This is straight confusion

I'm fightin' off the devil's illusions

And with everything I'm goin' through I feel like I'm
    losin' my mind

Because of time - it don't stop

It don't wait for no man

My schedule is packed

I feel like I'm in quickstand and sinkin' fast

The sand is at my chest and I'm too afraid to move

Because if I move it might be my doom

The only choice I have left is to trust God

But how could God still love me?

After feelin' like I could stand on my own two feet

I'm learnin' apart from God you can do nothin'

You can act like you got it together, but the truth is
    you don't

You can say that this weed and drink will make it
    better, but the truth is it won't

Nate Robinson

I can't front no more with mine

I need your help

But I want to know you for you - for myself

How do I achieve what's in my heart?

These ain't just words on paper

This is what's goin' on inside the mind of someone's
    life that only amounts to a vapor

Because this life can be here today and gone
    tomorrow

So many of us carry around unforgiven sorrow and
    we're gettin' hollow

Because we carry these secret emotions inside and
    don't let them out

When they locked up they get hard and that's what
    happens to our hearts

They get hard

But God has the key to set us all free

The only problem is I feel like I don't even believe
    me

God let me know that you're real again

    Come and sit down in the room and talk

You can be my only friend - til the end

Because of sin I feel that the love you have for me
    can never be the same

Please wipe away my shame and call on my name

If you can mold me?

If I can survive the fire?

Build my faith as high as the empire state and
  higher

Because of my geniuine desire to know the truth
  and to tell others

Make my crooked pathway straight

And please help me meet my mate

I hear her voice, but want evidence

I'm forced to wait and believe she'll be heaven sent

I got the money for your rent

Then you told me it was free

You said the blood covers every fee

You said just believe in me in your time of need

Because I have planted my seed and want to see it
  grow

You said you knew me before I was in the womb

And you will take control of my life until the tomb -
  if I let you

Well Lord, I don't have the strength anymore

I beg you to please open up heavens door

I want a blessin' from my Creator because that's
  what I've been waitin' for

You know my heart

You've seen my tears both seen and unseen

Please hold me close because a hug from you is all
  I need

                               Nate Robinson

Right/wrong

01/24/2001

Come one come all

To watch these facts fall

Like fat hard raindrops on the backspin of my
    basketball

You can't change the way the world turns

You can't make sure the wicked get what they
    deserve

You can't take other peoples' opinions and make
    them yours

You gotta find out what you believe and hope you
    have the strength to endure

The uncontrollable raging waters of life beating
    against your beach

At the same time being stressed with so many
    different directions to choose from

When will it end?

Only you have the final say to which directions get
    impeached

From beginning to end you are in a war

It don't make it any easier with other people
    fightin' to reach the same door

From philosphers to religions all the way down to
    an atheist

Who's to say who's right and who's wrong?

According to Christianity the world could end
tomorrow

   And over half the population would be in hell
dead and gone

Somebody help this lost and dyin' breed

   We all losin' our minds down here

Real flesh is bein' sacrificed because of greed

Grew up in the suburb, yet still these eyes have
seen too much pain

I've got daggers in my heart from betrayal and
confusion

Thought I had it together, but now it seems like an
illusion

I'm seein' walkin' mummies weighed down with
stress and disappointment

Most turn to drugs, sex, and anger for some
temporary enjoyment

When will we face it we all are tryin' to fill a void?

But the fact that you've tried just about everything
is something you can't avoid

Do I have the answer?

No, I'm just as lost as you

I'm just tryin' to make sense of everything, but
what is there to conclude?

That we live, then we die, and nothin' else matters
in between?

                                       Nate Robinson

I just can't accept that as fact - man, I'm stuck in a
   dream

I was brought up to believe that there is such a
   thing called sin

And if you commit it than hell will be your eternal
   end

So sin was something that I feared

Until I couldn't take it anymore because what I
   knew as life - suddenly veered

It still isn't clear in my mind what happened

I found myself all alone in church rappin'

Left once again with a huge mountain to climb

Believin' in the end his light will find a way to shine

The world we live in

02/27/2001

As I take a break from my everyday routine

So I can sit down and reflect on what's ahead for
me

Reality is something that we all must face

It's not good enough to just come in second place

In the back of my mind I know the truth

That all my life I can't be a youth

I gotta do what I can to prepare for what's comin'

A lifetime of workin' a 9 to 5 so ain't no use in
runnin'

But there's somethin' in my heart that won't let me
give up

When I'm tryin' so hard to not worry about what
other people want me to live up to

Tell me who can I turn to when my mind and
dreams are shattered?

Because of what I've been through I have so much
emotional stress

That I can't even remember who and what to
address

This test is nothing short of pain and misery

Knowin' that I live to die, but tryin' to find some
beauty in-between

     Nate Robinson

It seems that everybody else is caught in they own
web

Cautiously maneuvering through life don't forget to
watch your step

The wrong move can end what you've worked so
hard for

So many people just settle because they don't
believe that they can score

But cannot ignore the frustration and hurt that we
all experience

I'm goin' crazy cause they try to play me and fade
me

But I'm still here because none of this is serious

Life or death which one is better?

Though invaded by moments of glory still the
question remains

How can I hold my life together?

Had to deal with so much stuff, man I'm just tired

When to find my purpose in life is all I've ever
desired

I'm bein' rendered unconscious from the toxins of
everyday livin'

Knowin' that bein' on top doesn't guarantee that
you're flawlessly winnin'

Sinnin' don't help

And because of the previous sentence neither does
wealth - when your health is taken away

Nobody can be perfect

So you strive to, but you'll never achieve

    And after answering some of my own questions

    And considering other people's suggestions

    I can see how someone can reach the conclusion

Which is really an illusion - that it is better to just take my leave

Who's to say who's been deceived and what's right to believe?

'Cause when it comes down to it we are all equal

It's because of people's opinions and theories that screw everything up

And people's pride and ego 'cause nobody wants to be a punk

With this in mind our whole world is sunk

The question is - can anything fix it?

Because we've dug a hole so deep and we ain't doin' nothin' else but sinkin'

Nate Robinson

My prayer to the man up above

03/27/2001

My prayer to the man up above ....

Even though I'm strugglin' down here with
   gratifying my flesh

Somewhere deep down in my soul I believe one
   day I'll be at rest

Not just with my outward appearance

But whole on the inside and out because you've
   become my assurance

This occurence marks the day that I'm free

Free from worryin'

   Free from doubt

Free from allowin' negativity to take my spirit out

Hold me close - as I hold you closer

Satisfied and humble with whatever you give me

'Cause I want to make the most of each and every
   second I spend on your creation called Earth

I've been searchin' for my self-worth since birth

It hurts 'cause I feel low as dirt due to
   circumstances that I put on myself

I know I'm takin' chances with my spiritual health

I know I've done things in my short lifetime that
   should warrant your belt

But all I hear is that you're still near

And that if I choose to follow you I got nothin' to
    fear

To stand clear and allow you to fight my battles for
    me

It's worked so far

Yet, I still can't see how you could love me when I
    just spit in your face?

Why you bled for me when I left you without a
    trace?

I'm not in your house but still think of this often

Where will my spirit go when I'm dead and gone
    and layin' in a coffin?

Havin' faith translates to havin' instant power at my
    disposal

To use to conquer fear and doubt that you haven't
    already made your proposal

A mapped out pre-plan that represents the
    blueprints for my life

Why is it so hard to just take your hints?

Why does the world I live in care so much about
    who has the most dead presidents?

Can't we all just get along?

I've been told and I know that in my darkest hour is
    when I turn to you

   With my head tilted back

   Because I won't except the facts

                                    Nate Robinson

I swear I give my life to you

'Cause what you created me to do is worth stickin'
    it through

Even when I can't see your purpose

what else do I have to look forward to than
    society's 9 to 5 average everyday work service?

Bondage
04/07/01

When will all the little things stop mattering to us?

When will we be able to unify without judging each
other and without the negative fuss?

'Cause very few are willing to adjust

So many are set in their ways and are too afraid to
be open minded to change

They're willing to call others blinded because all
different ways of thinking seem strange

How can we as a people break ourselves free from
these chains?

These chains - oh these chains

They hold us captive and try to eliminate all
individual imagination and creativity

They cause anger, hate, and frustration

They confuse us, they blind us, they scare us
internally

What will it take to break us free?

Us represents those that dare to ask questions

Us represents those who live off of other people's
suggestions

Us represents those who've lost all hope

Us represents those who've taken their own lives
because they could not cope with no hope

                                        Nate Robinson

Free us - free us from this cage called the system

In these chains we rot and die with ideas and
    solutions that don't reach the surface

Because not only must we break these chains, but
    we must pick the lock for our cage

To be free is to have inner peace, yet it's not that
    simple

Every time we are told no or held back because of
    this system in our mind forms another ripple

What the ripple does is create cracks that only the
    truth can heal

I've searched high and low, but only the one who
    said, "I am the truth, the way, and the light."

Is what I've found to call real

We in the war zone called earth

We are all related through at least one thing - hurt

The struggle to free your mind is what represents
    the chains

But before that can happen you need to be one
    with the one who has the planet by the reigns

There's a brighter day comin' - is a guess

Because not one dead person I've known has ever
    come back to tell me its address

Unless the test is to withstand the constant pain?

Because when it comes down to it most live to
    increase their personal gain

This ain't a game

So don't laugh cause they ain't playin'

You only get one chance at this

With no guarantees - so it's wise to have a purpose

Where can you find it I don't know?

Yet I trust that when I'm ready the Lord won't
    hesitate to show

                                          Nate Robinson

Shoot for the stars

01/31/2001

Destiny, oh my Lord, what is destiny?

Who am I destined to be?

Regardless of what other people want to see from
me or who they want me to be

What is the gift you've given me?

What lies on the inside of this heart that loves the
beats?

Studied the streets and wants more than anything
else to be real

    Ain't too concerned about the money

    Ain't trippin' bout drivin' fancy cars or havin' the
finer things

I just wanna be real

To feel to touch to see people change

To be a part of uniting a group of people

To lead to experience to overthrow religion

I will go against the grain and dare to wait and have
faith that I have a destiny

Something that not one person can take from me

Something that will shine for all men to see

Shine bright

Be a light to fight with all my might

To allow myself to be used by God

And not to put any limitations on what he can do
    for me

When I was young I wanted to play in the NBA - to
    change the world

When we grow up - we lose our dreams

I choose not to lose my hope for a miracle

Big dreams are all we have left

I want to change the world - still

I lost it, but now I'm findin' it again

Still sometimes hard to stay away from sin

But he died so I could have the chance to win

Save me oh God from this torture called livin'

I can't see my future it's too dark

Even when I'm weak you remain strong

You will never leave me nor forsake me and you've
    forgiven every wrong

It's because of this I rely on you

    And when I'm down and out

Who else can I turn to but you? Pull me through

                          Nate Robinson

BE YOU

05/17/2003

From the deepest and darkest places come forth
the most fruitful and blessed things that have
ever been seen

We judge each other and separate ourselves over
appearance

And we forget about and completely ignore the
thing that connects us to each other and that
matters the most - our hearts

Invisible barriers that some will not allow to be
broken

While endless amounts of people suffer the global
effect - by chokin'

What ever happened to the power and strength in
hopin'?

Because a lot of people look down upon and
neglect the uniqueness of the token - 'X'

What will it take to break the fake who constantly
try to take - instead of give

When will jealousy and envy die?

So the rest of us can find out what it truly means to
live

Can I please go somewhere and not be judged for
holdin' hands with a woman who is not my skin
color?

Isn't love all that matters?

No it's all about greed and pride and no one can be
    "the one"

Or is it that everyone is trying to be "the one?"

When only unity gets every job done

We all need each other to survive

But many cannot forgive and forget

So Martin Luther King's dream sometimes seems
    that it may never fully come alive

I write words because words help me to express
    the way I feel inside

Most of us are taught that when we feel
    uncomfortable that the best thing to do with
    our emotions is to hide

While most everyone else hides behind their pride

Don't ever judge a book by its cover because you
    never know what's underneath

What always looks like trouble may represent what
    needs to happen for all of us to reach peace

CHANGE

What is it going to take for most of us to change?

To change the way we view people

To admit that we too have faults

To show vulnerability

To give someone else the combination to our
    forever locked vaults

                                    Nate Robinson

I believe that God holds the key to truly set the
human mind, body, and spirit free

But if we are too proud to see that the purpose of
life is to find our individual destiny

Love will eventually conquer hate on any occasion

And it's gonna take love from one person to the
next to win the battle of hate that we are all
facin'

As if it were a pure invasion

Can you be real with yourself?

Can you accept yourself for who you are?

Can you try to accept others for who they are?

Can you love yourself?

Because the plank must come out of your eye
before you can take the speck out of another

We don't have to be anybody else but who we are

Why can't some people see that?

We were not created to be the same

We were created to be different

And difference is something to celebrate not
something to be afraid of

Out of the darkest place can come the most
beautiful thing

But you must be able to open your eyes and ears

To see the door when it opens and to answer the
phone when it rings

My Life's Journey…

This life is not about things

It's about finding out what separates you and
connects you to others

It's about what makes you a human being

And if you can find out your purpose for being on
this earth

Then you will give yourself the best chance of living
a fulfilled life before your body returns to dirt

                                    Nate Robinson

The summary

07/02/2001

How can one cope with this isolation that I'm
constantly facin'?

Because there's no erasin' to my past hurts and
current frustrations

Although I'm patiently and impatiently waitin' for
God to move

I feel like I'm fightin' battles with satan and I lose

With all my dreams, ambition, and aspiration tell
me which path do I choose

While always askin' myself the question, can I win if
I break the rules?

Which brings me to my crossroads

Do I attempt to wait and trust in God knowin' I'm
movin' slow as the toad?

Or do I try and do it on my own like the hare
knowin' I can't rely on people to always be
there?

In this life, I wanna love the people that love me

I wanna love and help change the people that hate
me

I wanna take time out to teach others just how
powerful true love can be

But for all this to happen, first I know that it starts
   on the inside of me

So many of us want to win in life - me too

Yet so few of us will find what we're lookin' for
   because we are too afraid of we'd have to go
   through

To win, what does it mean to win?

To sin, what's so wrong with sin?

I understand you can only win within

'Cause, "If you ain't enough without it, you'll never
   be enough with it."

Get it?

Dreams, how I love to dream

Can you dare to dream?

'Cause it's so scary to dream

To dream of something different - to dream of
   change

To dare to think it could happen to most people
   seems strange

I am a dreamer and dreamin' gives my world range

Life's too short to go through it and not question

The hard part is finding facts to challenge all of
   their suggestions

Opinions, ones that they call facts

'Cause they too can bleed from the swing of an ax

We're mortal we all have to face death

                                    Nate Robinson

Knowin' that I have to die sometimes makes me
think that ain't nothin' left

What's good in this world one day can be corrupted
the next

So many people have lived and died all that lives on
is his text

Knowin' the truth is just the first step

Bein' able to act on your faith effectively is the
reason why only so few are kept

I hurt, don't you?

What keeps us apart is somethin' that's as visible as
dew

You might can smell it but it's hard to see

'Cause it's not about what's on the outside but
what's underneath

Here, take a peek

A lot are weak but act strong

It comes from havin' too many deep rooted weeds
planted in your lawn

Now keep in mind that these are just my guesses

And I still haven't found the answer to most of my
questions

But it's better to try than to not try at all

'Cause either way you look at it you're gonna fall

So I'll be in the cut movin' like the toad

Believin' I'll come through the fire as refined gold

My story's told - **BE BOLD**.

CPSIA information can be obtained at www.ICGtesting.com
Printed in the USA
BVOW03s1302260814

364227BV00004B/44/P